Your first 100 words in

ARABIC

Beginner's Quick & Easy Guide to Demystifying Arabic Script

Series concept
Jane Wightwick

Illustrations
Mahmoud Gaafar

Arabic edition
Mahmoud Gaafar

McGraw Hill

New York   Chicago   San Francisco   Lisbon   London   Madrid   Mexico City
Milan   New Delhi   San Juan   Seoul   Singapore   Sydney   Toronto

Audio CD edition
The accompanying CD contains three tracks for each topic:

Repeat and Remember
Speak and Understand
Test Yourself

Topics: 1 Around the House (tracks 2–4), 2 Clothes (tracks 5–7), 3 Around Town (tracks 8–10), 4 Countryside (tracks 11–13), 5 Opposites (tracks 14–16), 6 Animals (tracks 17–19), 7 Parts of the Body (tracks 20–22), 8 Useful Expressions (tracks 23–25), Round-Up (tracks 26–29)

4 5 6 7 8 9 10 11 12 13 14 15 16 17 18 CUS CUS 13 12 11 10 09

ISBN 978-0-8442-2395-7 (book)
MHID 0-8442-2395-6 (book)

ISBN 978-0-07-146928-9 (book & CD set)
MHID 0-07-146928-1 (book & CD set)

ISBN 978-0-07-146929-6 (book part of set)
MHID 0-07-146929-X (book part of set)

Library of Congress Control Number: 2006921331

McGraw-Hill books are available at special quantity discounts to use as premiums and sales promotions or for use in corporate training programs. To contact a representative, please visit the Contact Us pages at www.mhprofessional.com.

Other titles in this series

Your First 100 Words in Chinese
Your First 100 Words in French
Your First 100 Words in German
Your First 100 Words in Greek
Your First 100 Words in Hebrew
Your First 100 Words in Hindi
Your First 100 Words in Italian
Your First 100 Words in Japanese
Your First 100 Words in Korean
Your First 100 Words in Korean, CD edition
Your First 100 Words in Pashto
Your First 100 Words in Persian
Your First 100 Words in Russian
Your First 100 Words in Spanish
Your First 100 Words in Spanish, CD edition
Your First 100 Words in Vietnamese

This book is printed on acid-free paper.

◎ CONTENTS

INTRODUCTION

In this activity book you'll find 100 key words for you to learn to read in Arabic. All of the activities are designed specifically for reading non-Latin script languages. Many of the activities are inspired by the kind of games used to teach children to read their own language: flashcards, matching games, memory games, joining exercises, etc. This is not only a more effective method of learning to read a new script, but also much more fun.

We've included a **Scriptbreaker** to get you started. This is a friendly introduction to the Arabic script that will give you tips on how to remember the letters.

Then you can move on to the eight **Topics**. Each topic presents essential words in large type. There is also a pronunciation guide so you know how to say the words. These words are also featured in the tear-out **Flashcard** section at the back of the book. When you've mastered the words, you can go on to try out the activities and games for that topic.

There's also a **Round-up** section to review all your new words and the **Answers** to all the activities to check yourself.

Follow this 4-step plan for maximum success:

1 Have a look at the key topic words with their pictures. Then tear out the flashcards and shuffle them. Put them Arabic side up. Try to remember what the word means and turn the card over to check with the English. When you can do this, cover the pronunciation and try to say the word and remember the meaning by looking at the Arabic script only.

2 Put the cards English side up and try to say the Arabic word. Try the cards again each day both ways around. (When you can remember a card for seven days in a row, you can file it.)

3 Try out the activities and games for each topic. This will re-inforce your recognition of the key words.

4 After you have covered all the topics, you can try the activities in the **Round-up** section to test your knowledge of all the 100 words in the book. You can also try shuffling all the flashcards together to see how many you can remember.

This flexible and fun way of reading your first words in Arabic should give you a head start whether you're learning at home or in a group.

◎ SCRIPTBREAKER

The purpose of this Scriptbreaker is to introduce you to the Arabic script and how it is formed. You should not try to memorize the alphabet at this stage, nor try to write them yourself. Instead, have a quick look through this section and then move on to the topics, glancing back if you want to work out the letters in a particular word. Remember, though, that recognizing the whole shape of the word in an unfamiliar script is just as important as knowing how it is made up. Using this method you will have a much more instinctive recall of vocabulary and will gain the confidence to expand your knowledge in other directions.

The Arabic script is not nearly as difficult as it might seem at first glance. There are 28 letters (only two more than in the English alphabet), no capital letters, and, unlike English, words are spelled as they sound. There are two main points to etch into your brain:

- Arabic is written from right to left.
- The letters are "joined up" — you cannot "print" a word as you can in English.

◎ The alphabet

The easiest way of tackling the alphabet is to divide it into similarly shaped letters. For example, here are two group of similar letters. The only difference between them is the dots:

ح (the letter *Haa*)   ب (the letter *baa*)

ج (the letter *jeem*)   ت (the letter *taa*)

خ (the letter *khaa*)   ث (the letter *thaa*)

When these letters join to other letters they change their shape. The most common change is that they lose their "tails":

$$ تج = ج + ت \qquad حب = ب + ح $$ (read from *right to left*)

Because letters change their shape like this, they have an *initial*, a *medial* (middle) and a *final* form. For example, the letter ج (*jeem*) changes like this:

at the beginning of a word (*initial*)   ...جـ

in the middle of a word (*medial*)   ...ـجـ...

at the end of a word (*final*)   ـج...

✔ Arabic has 28 letters and no capital letters

✔ Arabic reads right to left

✔ Arabic is written in "joined up" writing

✔ The "tail" is generally chopped off before joining to the next letter

A few letters change their shapes completely depending on where they fall in a word. For example, the letter ه (*haa*) changes like this:

initial	ـهـ...
medial	...ـهـ...
final	ـه...

In addition, there are six letters which *never* join to the letter *following* (to their left) and so hardly change shape at all. These are:

و (*waw*)   ا (*alif*)

د (*daal*)   ذ (*THaal*)

ر (*raa*)   ز (*zay*)

You will find more details of how the individual letters change their shape in the table on page 8.

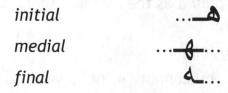 Formation of words

We can use the principles of joining letters to form words.

So, for example, the Arabic word for "river" (*nahr*) is written like this:

(*nahr*) نهر = (r) ر + (h) ه + (n) ن ⟵

The Arabic word for "belt" (Ḥizaam), contains two non-joining letters and is written like this:

(Ḥizaam) حزام = (m) م + (aa) ا + (z) ز + (Ḥ) ح ⟵

You may have noticed that some of the vowels seem to be missing from the script. In written Arabic, the three short vowels (*a, i, u*) are not written as part of the script but as vowel signs above or below the letter. The short *a* is written as a dash above the letter (ˊ); the short *i* as a dash below (ˎ); and the short *u* as a comma-shape above (ˀ). This is similar to English shorthand, where we might write "bnk" instead of "bank." Here are the words for "river" and "belt" again, this time with the vowel signs:

نَهر (nahr) حِزام (Hizaam)

In this book we have included these vowel signs in the topics, but dropped them in the review section (*Round-up*). Most material for native speakers will leave them out as you are presumed to know them. This makes it all the more important for you to start recognizing a word without the short vowels.

✔ Arabic letters have an *initial*, *medial* ("middle") and *final* form, depending on their position in the word

✔ Many Arabic letters simply lose their tails for the *medial* and *final* form

✔ A few letters change their shape completely

✔ 6 letters don't join to the letter after and hardly change at all

✔ The short vowels (*a*, *i*, *u*) are written as vowel signs above and below the letter and are not usually included in modern written Arabic

Pronunciation tips

This activity book has simplified some aspects of pronunciation in order to emphasize the basics. Don't worry at this stage about being precisely correct – the other letters in a word will help you to be understood. Many Arabic letters are pronounced in a similar way to their English equivalents, but here are a few that need special attention:

ص (saad) a strong "s," pronounced with the tongue on the roof of the mouth rather than up against the teeth

ض (Daad) a strong "d," pronounced with the tongue on the roof of the mouth rather than up against the teeth

ط (*таа*)	a strong "t," pronounced with the tongue on the roof of the mouth rather than up against the teeth	
ظ (*zaa*)	a strong "z," pronounced with the tongue on the roof of the mouth rather than up against the teeth	
ح (*наа*)	pronounced as a breathy "h"	
خ (*khaa*)	pronounced like the "ch" in the Yiddish "chutzpah"	
ع (*'ayn*)	the sound most often associated with Arabic, and most difficult to produce: a sort of guttural "ah"-sound	
غ (*ghayn*)	pronounced like the French throaty "r"	
ء (*hamza*)	a strange "half letter." Not really pronounced at all, but has the effect of cutting short the previous letter	
ة (*taa marboota*)	a version of (*taa*) that only appears at the end of words and is pronounced "a"	

Summary of the Arabic alphabet

The table below shows all the Arabic letters in the three positions, with the Arabic letter name, followed by the sound. Remember that this is just for reference and you shouldn't expect to take it all in at once. If you know the basic principles of how the Arabic script works, you will slowly come to recognize the individual letters.

	initial:	medial:	final:		initial:	medial:	final:		initial:	medial:	final:
alif *a/u/i/aa*	ا	ـا	ـا	zaa *z*	ز	ـز	ـز	qaaf *q*	ق	ـقـ	ـق
baa *b*	بـ	ـبـ	ـب	seen *s*	سـ	ـسـ	ـس	kaaf *k*	كـ	ـكـ	ـك
taa *t*	تـ	ـتـ	ـت	sheen *sh*	شـ	ـشـ	ـش	laam *l*	لـ	ـلـ	ـل
thaa *th*	ثـ	ـثـ	ـث	saad *s*	صـ	ـصـ	ـص	meem *m*	مـ	ـمـ	ـم
jaa *j*	جـ	ـجـ	ـج	Daad *D*	ضـ	ـضـ	ـض	noon *n*	نـ	ـنـ	ـن
наа *H*	حـ	ـحـ	ـح	Taa *T*	طـ	ـطـ	ـط	haa *h*	هـ	ـهـ	ـه
khaa *kh*	خـ	ـخـ	ـخ	zaa *z*	ظـ	ـظـ	ـظ	waaw *w/oo*	و	ـو	ـو
daal *d*	د	ـد	ـد	'ayn *'*	عـ	ـعـ	ـع	yaa *y/ee*	يـ	ـيـ	ـي
THaal *TH*	ذ	ـذ	ـذ	ghayn *gh*	غـ	ـغـ	ـغ				
raa *r*	ر	ـر	ـر	faa *f*	فـ	ـفـ	ـف				

① AROUND THE HOME

Look at the pictures of things you might find in a house.
Tear out the flashcards for this topic.
Follow steps 1 and 2 of the plan in the introduction.

شُبّاك
shubbaak

كُرسي
kursee

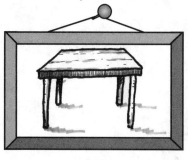

مائِدة
maa-ida

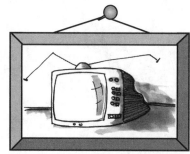

تِليفزيون
tileefizyoon

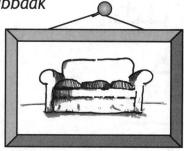

كَنَبة *kanaba*

كُمبيوتر
kumbiyootir

تِليفون
tileefoon

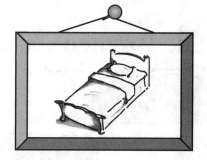

سَرير
sareer

ثَلاجة
thallaaja

دولاب
doolaab

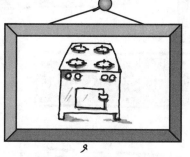

فُرن *furn*

باب
baab

◎ **M**atch the pictures with the words, as in the example.

كَنَبة
سَرير
شُباك
مائِدة
تِليفِزيون
كُرسي
كُمبيوتر
تِليفون

◎ **N**ow match the Arabic household words to the English.

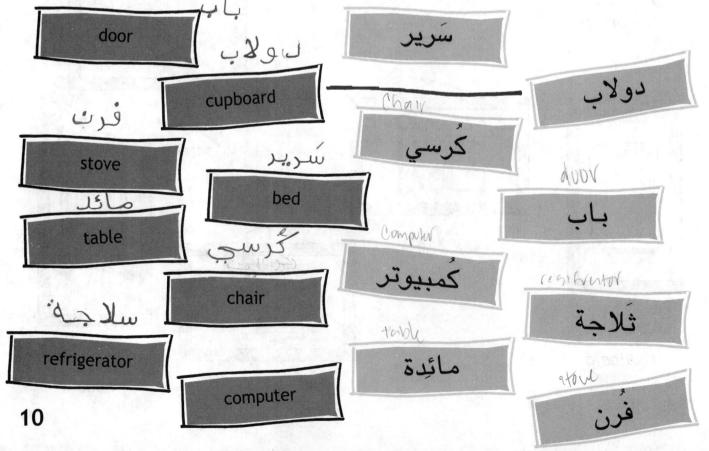

door

باب

cupboard

دولاب

Chair

كُرسي

فرن

stove

door

مائد

باب

bed

سَرير

table

Computar

كُرسي

كُمبيوتر

chair

resigvutor

ثلاجة

سلاجة

table

refrigerator

مائِدة

computer

stove

فُرن

◎ **M**atch the words and their pronunciation.

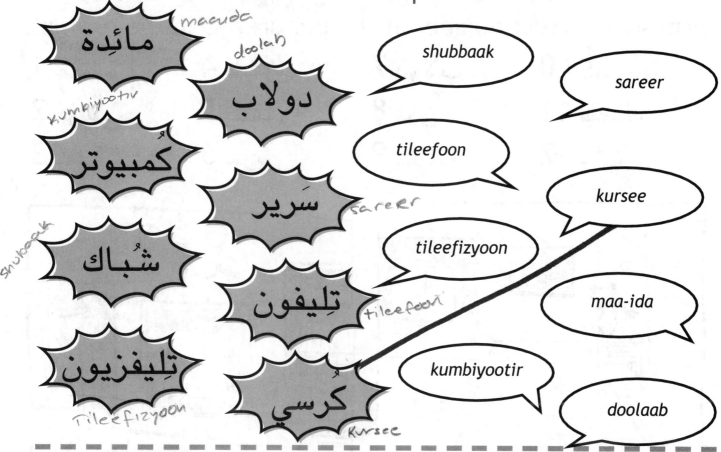

- -

◎ **S**ee if you can find these words in the word square.

The words run *right to left*.

فُرن

سَرير

كُرسي

ثَلاجة

باب

كَنَبة

ذ	و	ح	ت	ر	ي	ر	س
ط	ة	ج	لا	ث	ش	ا	ف
د	ه	ت	ز	ل	خ	د	ث
ة	ب	ن	ك	ف	ق	و	ظ
ك	ف	ي	س	ر	ك	ي	م
ن	ي	ا	ج	س	ن	ع	ط
ع	ن	ر	ف	ة	ذ	ف	و
ث	ف	ف	ة	غ	ح	ا	ب

11

Decide where the household items should go. Then write the correct number in the picture, as in the example.

10 كُمبيوتر	7 دولاب	4 تِليفزيون	1 مائِدة
11 شُباك	8 فُرن	5 تِليفون	2 كُرسي
12 باب	9 ثَلاجة	6 سَرير	3 كَنَبة

Now see if you can fill in the household word at the bottom of the page by choosing the correct Arabic.

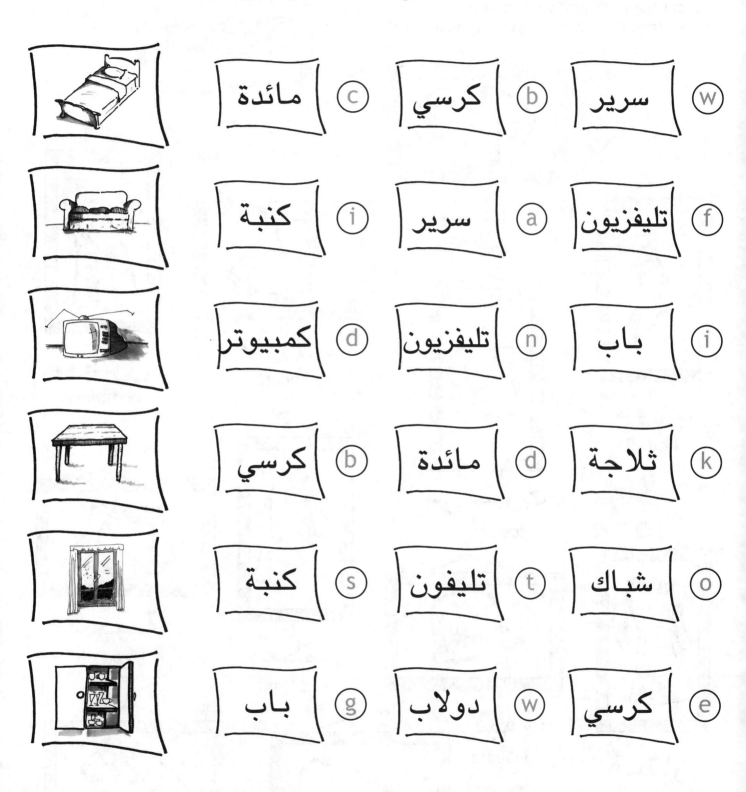

English word: ⓦ ◯ ◯ ◯ ◯ ◯

❷ CLOTHES

Look at the pictures of different clothes.
Tear out the flashcards for this topic.
Follow steps 1 and 2 of the plan in the introduction.

حِزام
Hizaam

بُلوفر
buloofir

شورت
shoort

بَنطَلون
banTaloon

جَورَب
jawrab

تي شيرت
tee-sheert

مِعطَف
mi'Taf

جيبة
jeeba

فُستان
fustaan

قُبَّعة
qubba'a

حِذاء *HiThaa*

قَميص *qamees*

14

Match the Arabic words and their pronunciation.

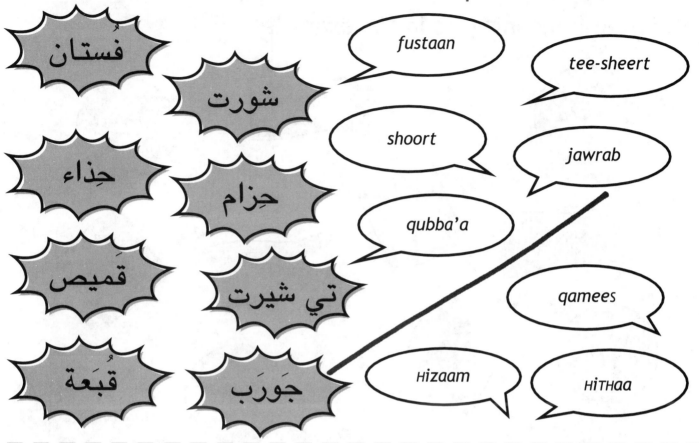

فُستان

شورت

حِذاء

حِزام

قَميص

تي شيرت

قُبَّعة

جَورَب

fustaan

tee-sheert

shoort

jawrab

qubba'a

qamees

ℋizaam

ℋiтнaa

- -

See if you can find these clothes in the word square.
The words run *right to left*.

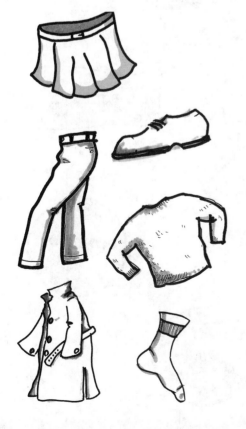

ق	ي	ث	ب	ل	و	ف	ر
ج	و	ر	ب	لا	ج	ة	ط
ث	د	خ	ل	ز	ت	هـ	د
ظ	و	ق	ف	ج	ي	ب	هـ
مـ	ي	خ	ر	سـ	ي	ف	ك
بـ	ن	ط	لـ	و	ن	يـ	ظ
و	فـ	مـ	عـ	طـ	فـ	ا	م
حـ	ذ	ا	ء	غـ	ة	فـ	ث

15

Now match the Arabic words, their pronunciation, and the English meaning, as in the example.

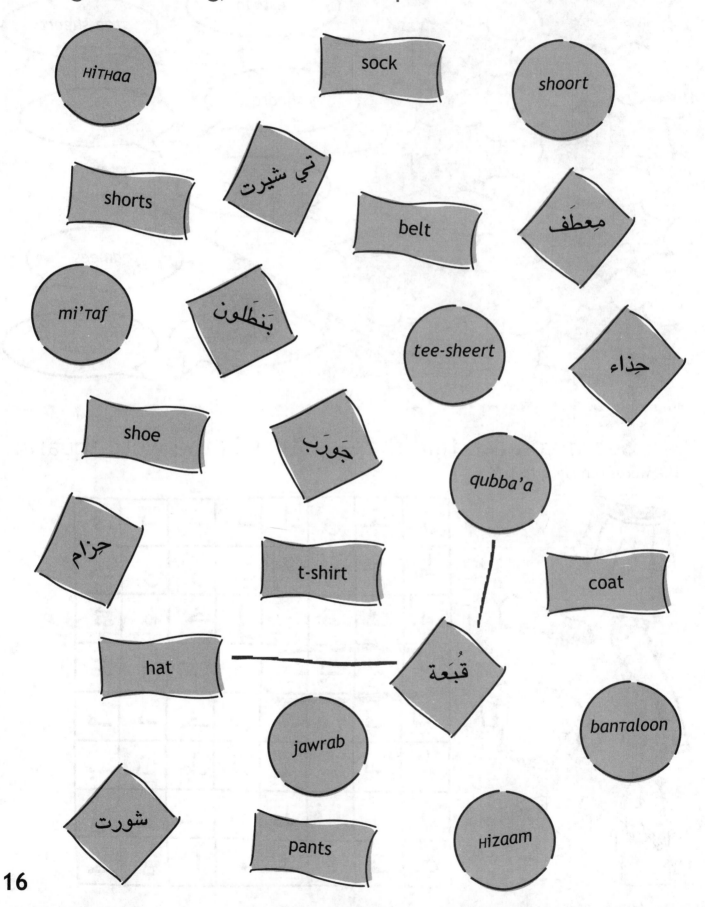

HiTHaa

sock

shoort

shorts

تي شيرت

belt

مِعطَف

mi'Taf

بنطَلون

tee-sheert

حِذاء

shoe

جَورَب

qubba'a

حِزام

t-shirt

coat

hat

قُبَّعة

banTaloon

jawrab

شورت

pants

Hizaam

◎ **C**andy is going on vacation. Count how many of each type of clothing she is packing in her suitcase.

	قبعة	2		معطف			حزام			حذاء	
	بنطلون			شورت			فستان			جورب	
	جيبة			تي شيرت			قميص			بلوفر	

Someone has ripped up the Arabic words for clothes.
Can you join the two halves of the words, as the example?

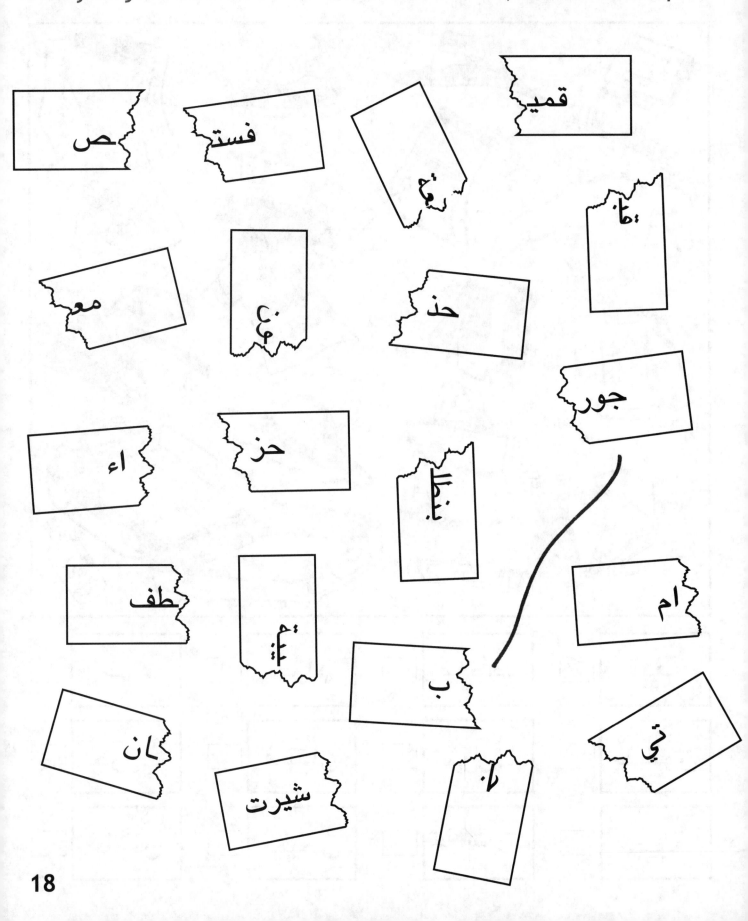

18

❸ AROUND TOWN

Look at the pictures of things you might find around town.
Tear out the flashcards for this topic.
Follow steps 1 and 2 of the plan in the introduction.

فُندُق

funduq

أُوتوبيس

ootoobees

بيت

bayt

سَيارة

sayyaara

سِينما

seenimaa

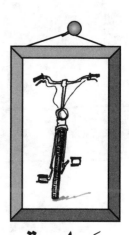

دَراجة

darraaja

قِطار

qiтaar

تاكسي *taaksee*

madrasa مَدرَسة

شارِع *shaari'*

مَحَل *maнall*

maт'am مطعَم

19

Ⓞ **M**atch the Arabic words to their English equivalents.

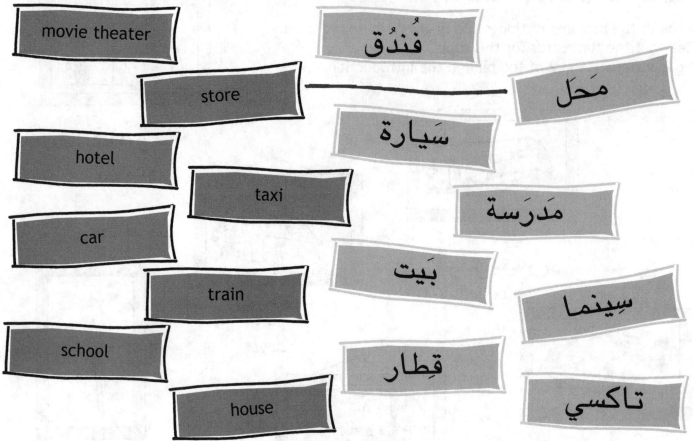

movie theater

فُندُق

store

مَحَل

سَيارة

hotel

taxi

مَدرَسة

car

بَيت

train

سِينما

school

قِطار

house

تاكسي

Ⓞ **N**ow list the correct order of the English words to match the Arabic word chain, as in the example.

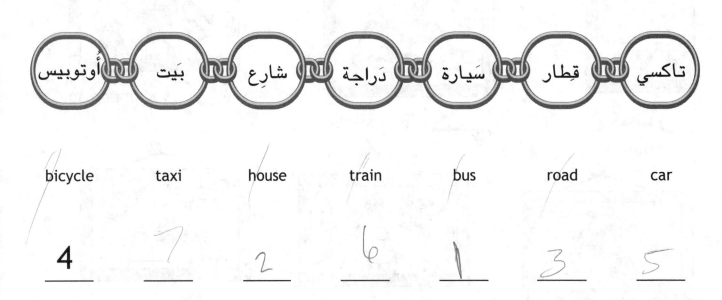

bicycle	taxi	house	train	bus	road	car
4	7	2	6	1	3	5

20

Match the words to the signs.

أُوتوبيس	دَراجة	سَيارة	مَدرَسة
تاكسي	فُندُق	قِطار	مَطعَم

Now choose the Arabic word that matches the picture to fill in the English word at the bottom of the page.

English word: (s) ( ) ( ) ( ) ( ) ( )

اوتوبيس

تاكسي

مَدرَسة

سَيارة

فُندُق

بَيت

دَراجة

قِطار

مَحَل

سِينما

مَطعَم

شارِع

bayt

ootoobees

qiтaar

maт'am

maнall

madrasa

taaksee

seenimaa

shaari'

funduq

sayyaara

darraaja

❹ COUNTRYSIDE

Look at the pictures of things you might find in the countryside.
Tear out the flashcards for this topic.
Follow steps 1 and 2 of the plan in the introduction.

تَل *tal*

جَبَل *jabal*

وَردة *warda*

غابة *ghaaba*

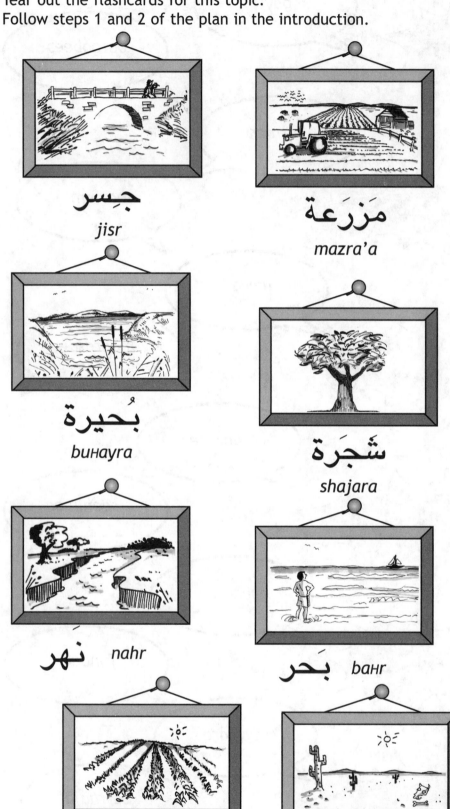

جِسر *jisr*

مَزرَعة *mazra'a*

بُحيرة *buнayra*

شَجَرة *shajara*

نَهر *nahr*

بَحر *baнr*

حَقل *нaql*

صَحراء *saнraa*

24

Can you match all the countryside words to the pictures?

جَبَل

مَزرَعة

بَحر

غابة

صَحراء

تَل

بُحيرة

جِسر

نَهر

وَردة

شَجَرة

حَقل

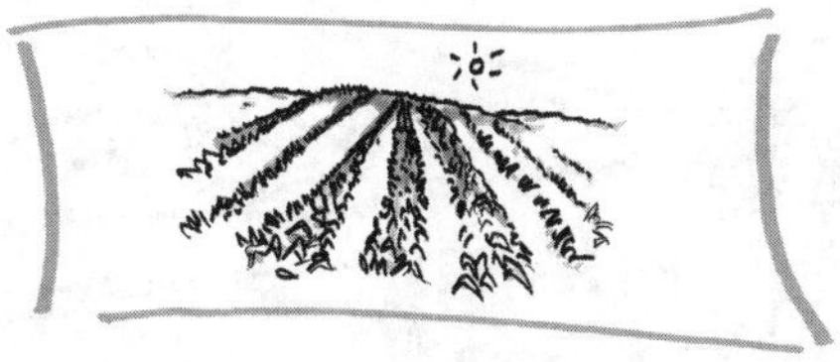

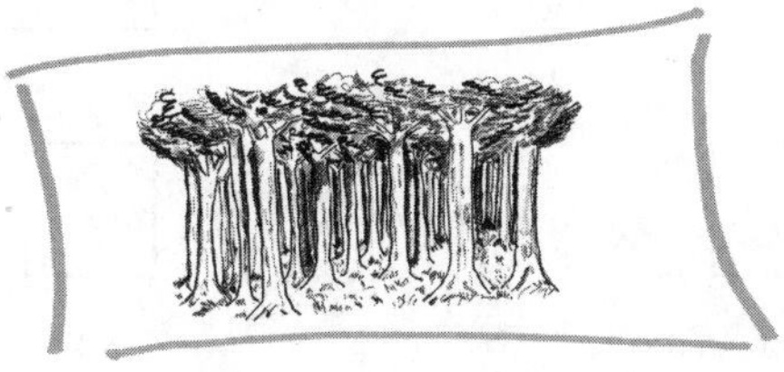

Now check (✔) the features you can find in this landscape.

جِسر ✔		شَجَرة ☐		صَحراء ☐	تَل ☐
جبَل ☐		بَحر ☐		حَقل ☐	غابة ☐
بُحيرة ☐		نَهر ☐		وَردة ☐	مَزرَعة ☐

26

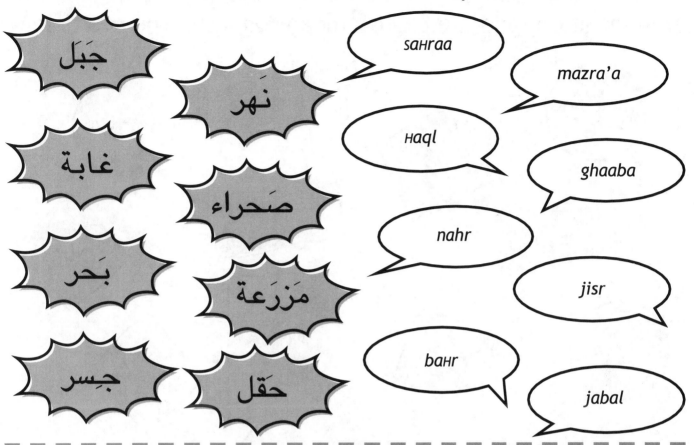

Match the Arabic words and their pronunciation.

◎ **See if you can find these words in the word square.**

The words run *right to left*.

ه	ف	و	س	ب	ث	ي	نـ
ة	ر	جـ	شـ	بـ	خـ	و	جـ
د	هـ	ـتـ	ة	د	ر	و	ثـ
ة	ر	يـ	ـحـ	بـ	قـ	و	ظـ
ق	ي	ة	ـعـ	ر	ز	مـ	ثـ
ف	نـ	يـ	و	بـ	ظـ	ل	تـ
م	ا	غ	ط	ـقـ	مـ	فـ	و
بـ	مـ	ر	ـسـ	جـ	ا	ذ	ضـ

شَجَرة

مَزرَعة

تَل

وَردة

جِسر

بُحيرة

27

Finally, test yourself by joining the Arabic words, their pronunciation, and the English meanings, as in the example.

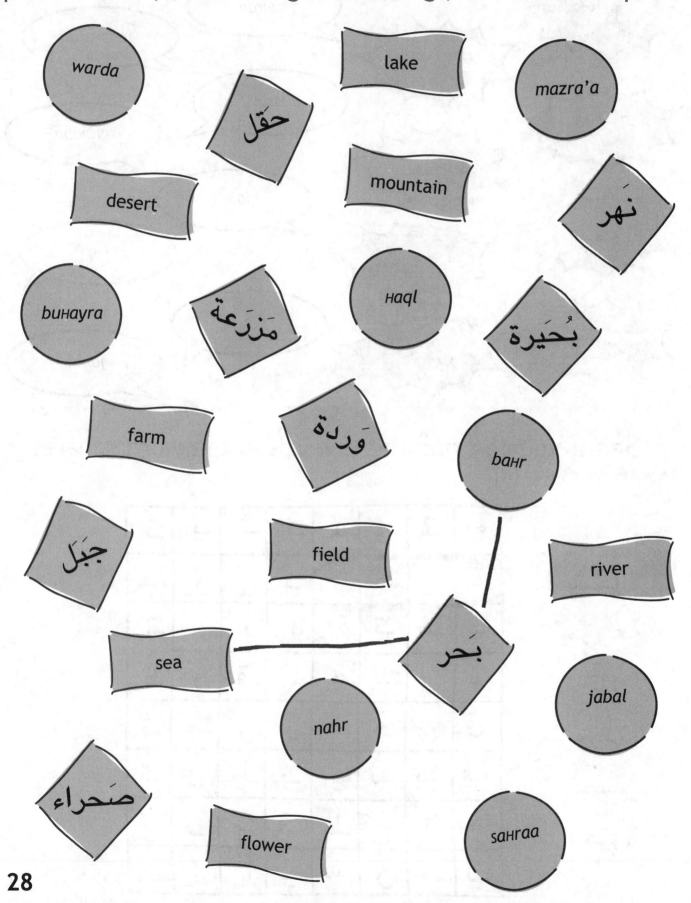

warda

lake

mazra'a

حَقل

desert

mountain

نَهر

buнayra

مَزرعة

наql

بُحَيرة

farm

وَردة

baнr

جَبَل

field

river

sea

بَحر

jabal

nahr

صَحراء

flower

saнraa

❺ OPPOSITES

Look at the pictures.
Tear out the flashcards for this topic.
Follow steps 1 and 2 of the plan in the introduction.

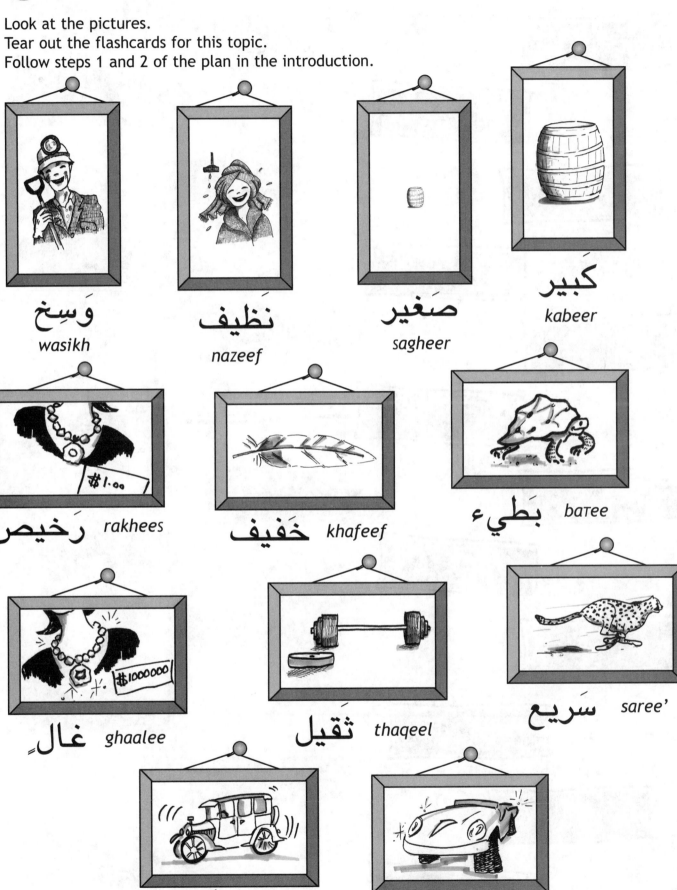

وَسِخ
wasikh

نَظيف
nazeef

صَغير
sagheer

كبير
kabeer

رَخيص
rakhees

خَفيف
khafeef

بَطيء
baтee

غالٍ
ghaalee

ثَقيل
thaqeel

سَريع
saree'

قَديم
qadeem

جَديد
jadeed

29

Join the Arabic words to their English equivalents.

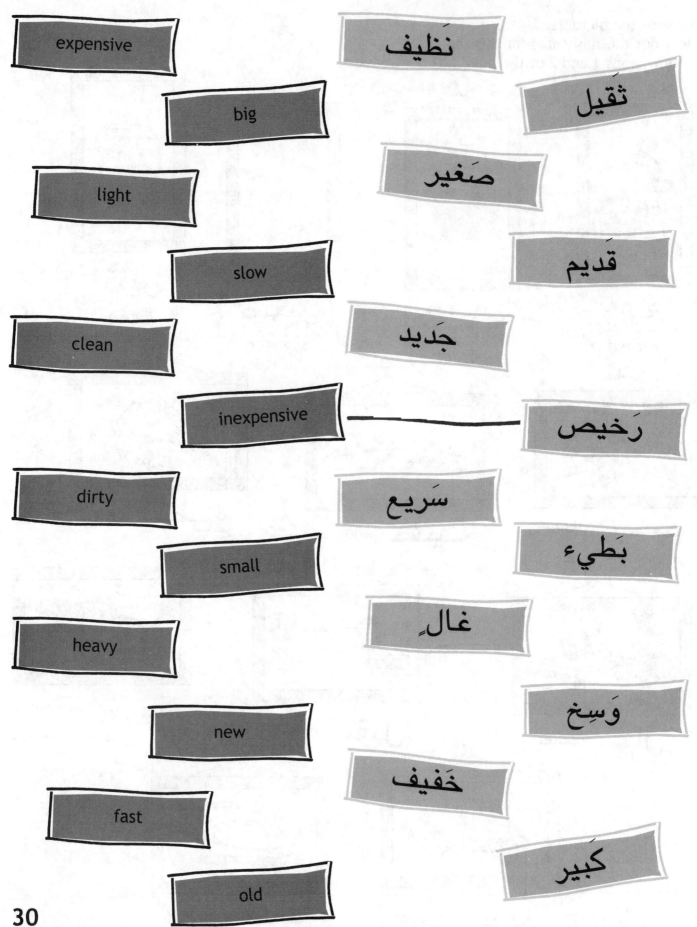

expensive

نَظيف

big

ثَقيل

light

صَغير

slow

قَديم

clean

جَديد

inexpensive ———————— رَخيص

dirty

سَريع

small

بَطيء

heavy

غالٍ

new

وَسِخ

fast

خَفيف

old

كَبير

Now choose the Arabic word that matches the picture to fill in the English word at the bottom of the page.

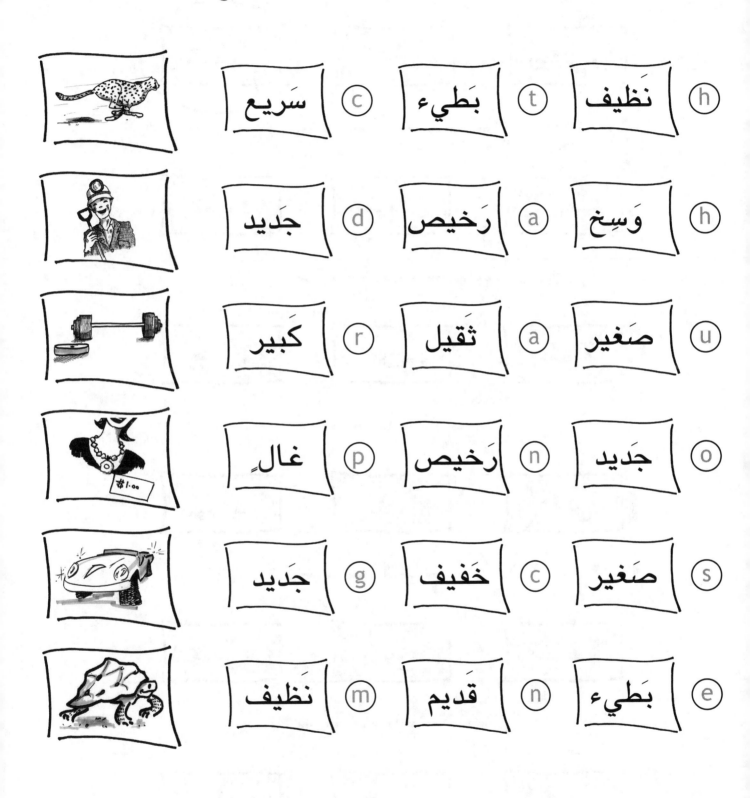

English word: ◯ ◯ ◯ ◯ ◯ ◯

Find the odd one out in these groups of words.

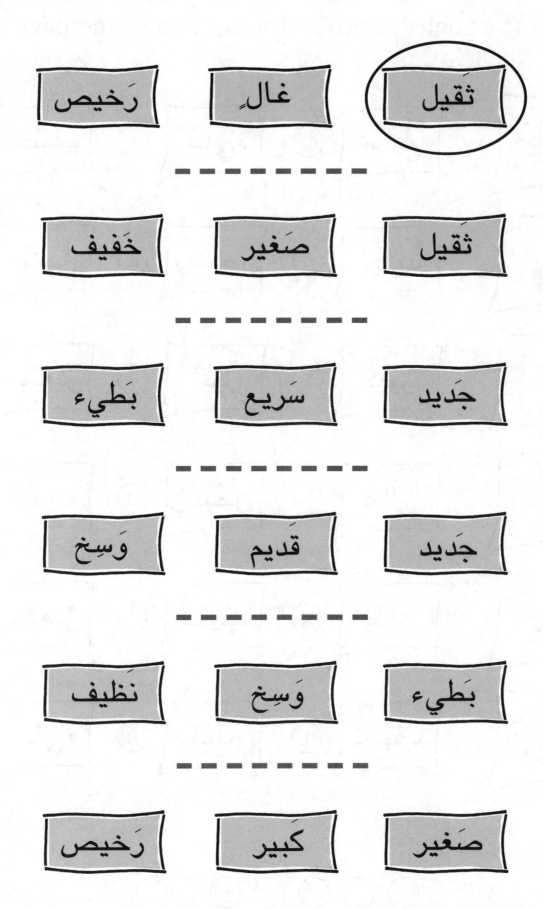

رَخيص	غالٍ	ثَقيل
خَفيف	صَغير	ثَقيل
بَطيء	سَريع	جَديد
وَسِخ	قَديم	جَديد
نَظيف	وَسِخ	بَطيء
رَخيص	كَبير	صَغير

© **F**inally, join the English words to their Arabic opposites, as in the example.

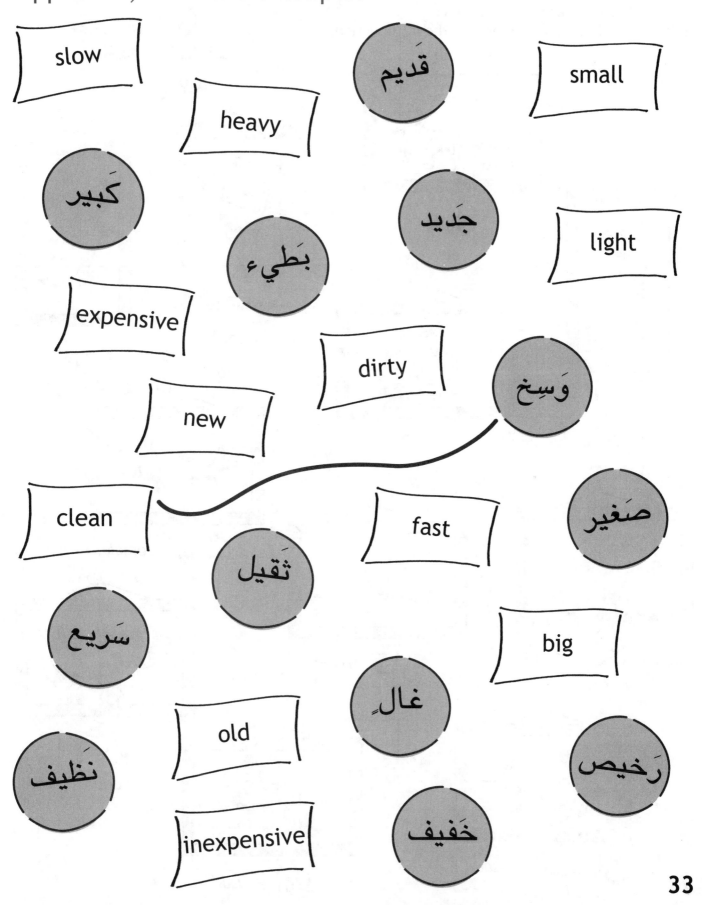

slow

قَديم

small

heavy

كَبير

جَديد

light

بَطيء

expensive

dirty

وَسِخ

new

صَغير

clean

fast

ثَقيل

سَريع

big

غالٍ

old

نَظيف

رَخيص

inexpensive

خَفيف

❻ ANIMALS

Look at the pictures.
Tear out the flashcards for this topic.
Follow steps 1 and 2 of the plan in the introduction.

بَطة
baTTa

فيل
feel

قِطة
qiTTa

كَلب
kalb

أرنَب
arnab

قِرد
qird

سَمكة
samaka

خَروف
kharoof

فأر
faar

بَقرة
baqara

حُصان
Husaan

أسَد
asad

Match the animals to their associated pictures, as in the example.

أرنَب

حُصان

قِرد

قِطة

خَروف

فأر

كَلب

أسَد

سَمَكة

بَقرة

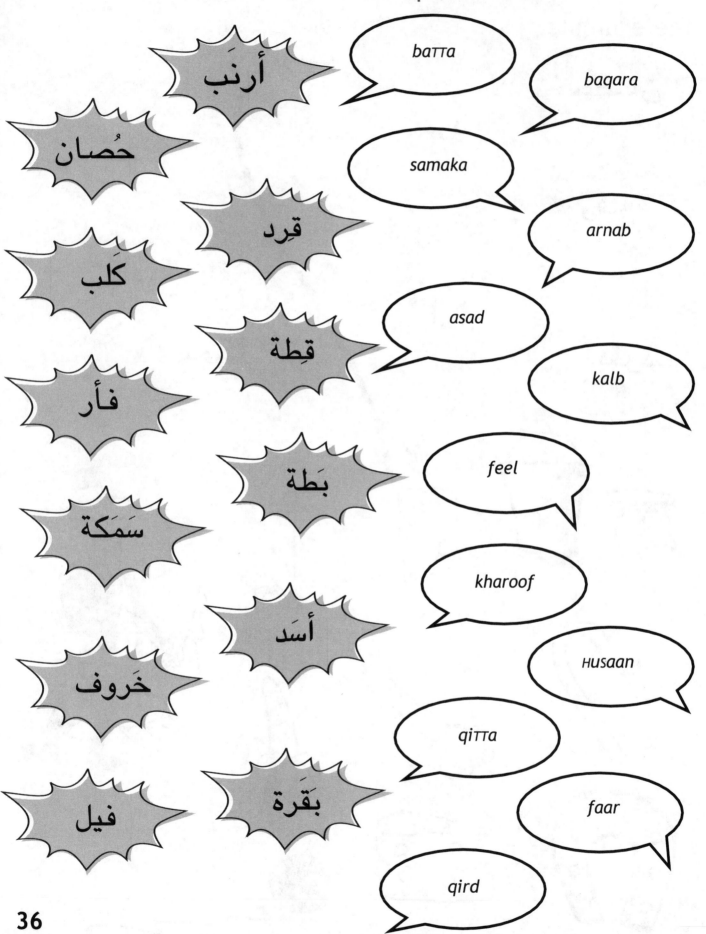

Check (✔) the animal words you can find in the word pile.

بُحَيرة   قِطة   كُرسي   سَيارة

أرنَب   فيل   خَروف   سَرير

ثَقيل   كَنَبة   سينما   حِذاء

تَل   أسَد   بَقَرة   سَمَكة

Join the Arabic animals to their English equivalents.

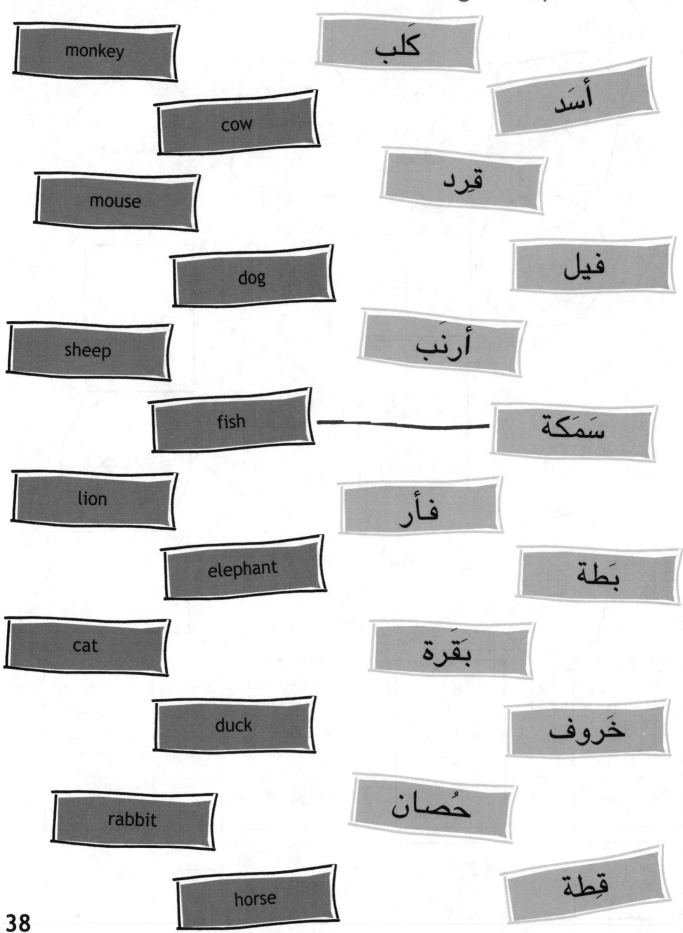

monkey

cow

mouse

dog

sheep

fish

lion

elephant

cat

duck

rabbit

horse

كَلب

أَسَد

قِرد

فيل

أَرنَب

سَمَكة

فأر

بَطة

بَقَرة

خَروف

حُصان

قِطة

7 PARTS OF THE BODY

Look at the pictures of parts of the body.
Tear out the flashcards for this topic.
Follow steps 1 and 2 of the plan in the introduction.

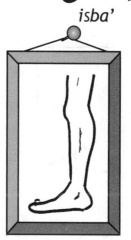
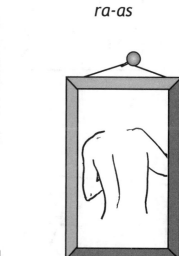

إِصبَع
isba'

رَأس
ra-as

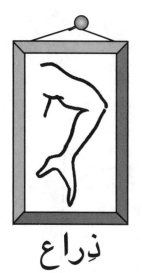

ذِراع
THiraa

عَين
'ayn

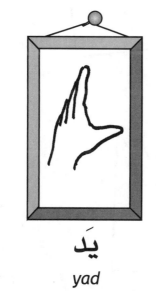

ساق
saaq

شَعر
sha'r

ظَهر
zahr

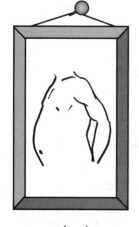

بَطن
baTn

يَد
yad

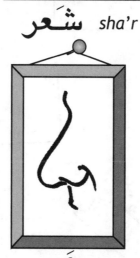

أُذُن
uTHun

أَنف
anf

فَم
fam

39

Someone has ripped up the Arabic words for parts of the body. Can you join the two halves of the word again?

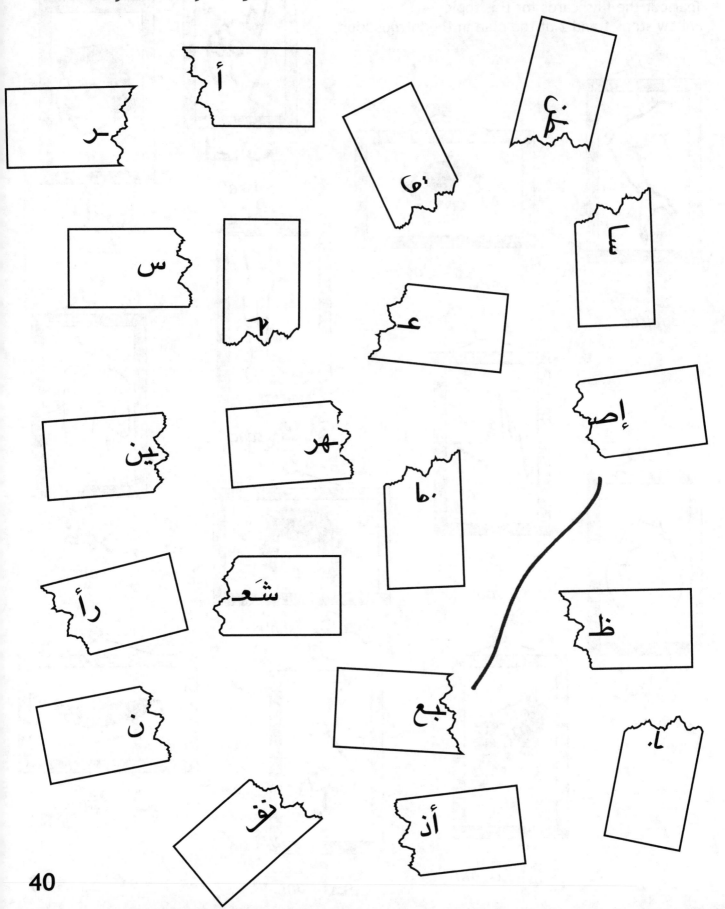

See if you can find and circle six parts of the body in the word square, then draw them in the boxes below.

The words run *right to left*.

ه	فـ	و	ســ	بـ	مـ	فـ	نـ
ة	ر	د	ج	و	مـ	حـ	مـ
د	ق	ا	ســ	د	ر	و	ثـ
ة	ر	ا	جـ	عـ	قـ	و	ظ
ة	نـ	يـ	ز	تـ	نـ	ذ	أ
ن	يـ	عـ	د	ر	شـ	ع	و
م	ا	فـ	نـ	أ	مـ	قـ	و
ب	ى	لـ	يـ	لـ	ا	ذ	ضـ

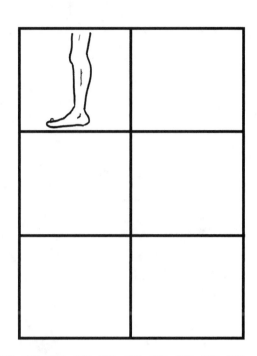

Now match the Arabic to the pronunciation.

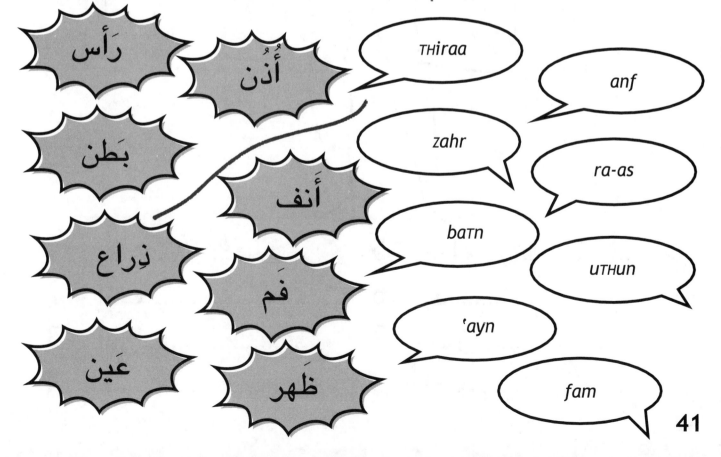

رَأْس   أُذن   THiraa   anf

بَطن   أَنف   zahr   ra-as

ذِراع   فَم   baTn   uTHun

عَين   ظَهر   'ayn   fam

Label the body with the correct number, and write the pronunciation next to the words.

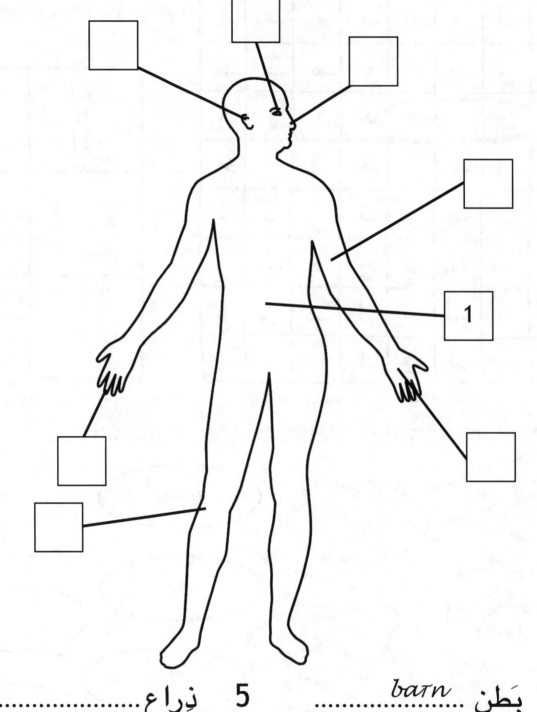

5	ذِراع	1	بَطن .... *baтn*
6	يَد	2	أنف ....
7	ساق	3	أُذُن ....
8	إصبَع	4	عَين ....

© **F**inally, match the Arabic words, their pronunciation, and the English meanings, as in the example.

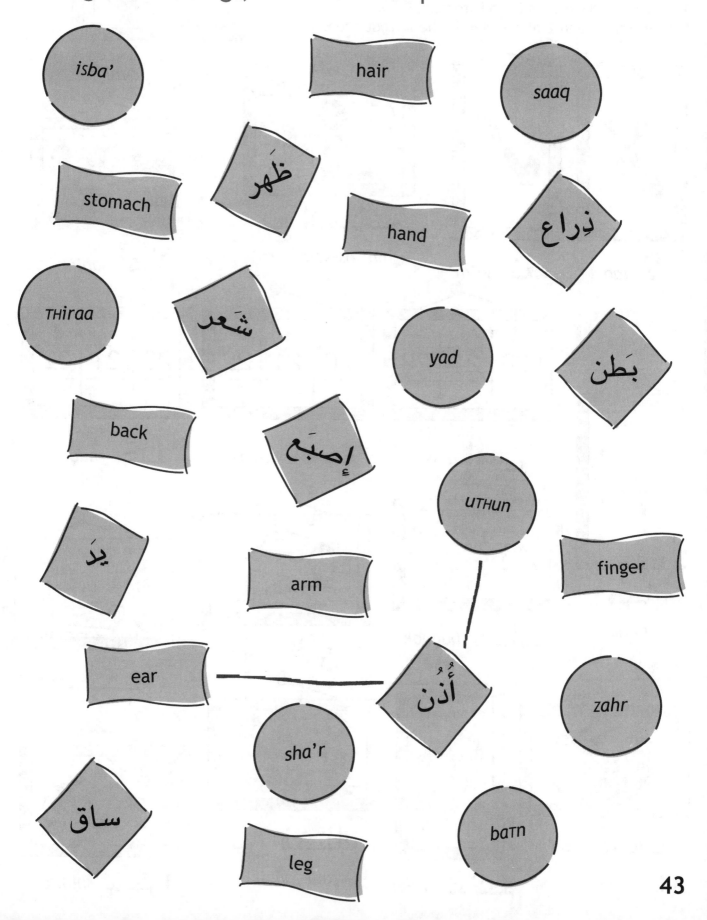

isba'

hair

saaq

ظَهر

stomach

hand

ذِراع

THiraa

شَعر

yad

بَطن

back

إصبَع

uTHun

يَد

finger

arm

ear

أُذُن

zahr

ساق

sha'r

baTn

leg

⑧ USEFUL EXPRESSIONS

Look at the pictures.
Tear out the flashcards for this topic.
Follow steps 1 and 2 of the plan in the introduction.

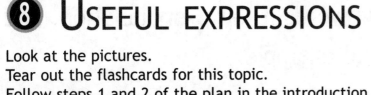

أَين؟ *ayn?*

مَع السَلامة
ma' as-salaama

أَهلا *ahlan*

لا *laa*

نَعَم *na'm*

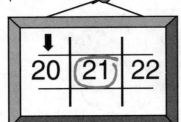

أَمس *ams*

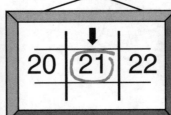

اليَوم *al-yawm*

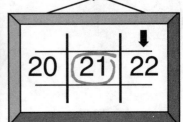

غَدا *ghadan*

هُنا
huna

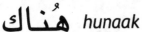

هُناك *hunaak*

الآن *al-aan*

بِكَم؟ *bikam?*

آسِف *aasif*

عَظيم *'azeem*

مِن فَضلَك
min faᴅlak

شُكرا *shukran*

44

Match the Arabic words to their English equivalents.

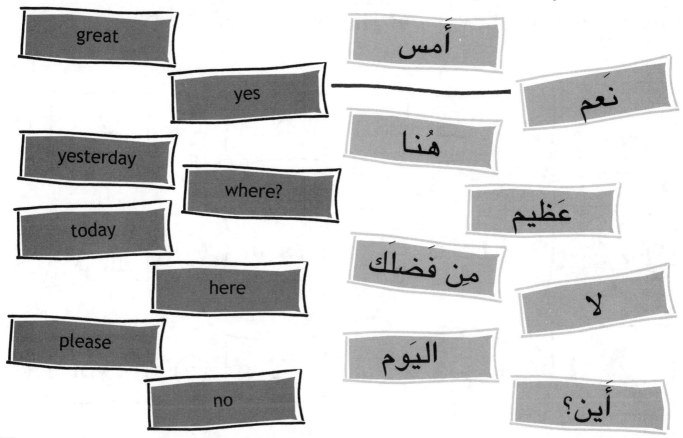

great

yes

yesterday

where?

today

here

please

no

أَمس

نَعَم

هُنا

عَظيم

مِن فَضلَك

لا

اليَوم

أَين؟

Now match the Arabic to the pronunciation.

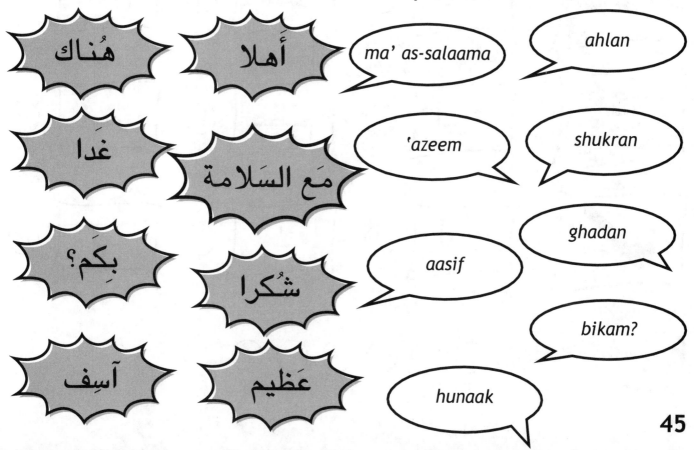

هُناك

أَهلا

ma' as-salaama

ahlan

غَدا

مَع السَلامة

'azeem

shukran

بِكَم؟

ghadan

aasif

شُكرا

آسِف

عَظيم

bikam?

hunaak

Choose the Arabic word that matches the picture to fill in the English word at the bottom of the page.

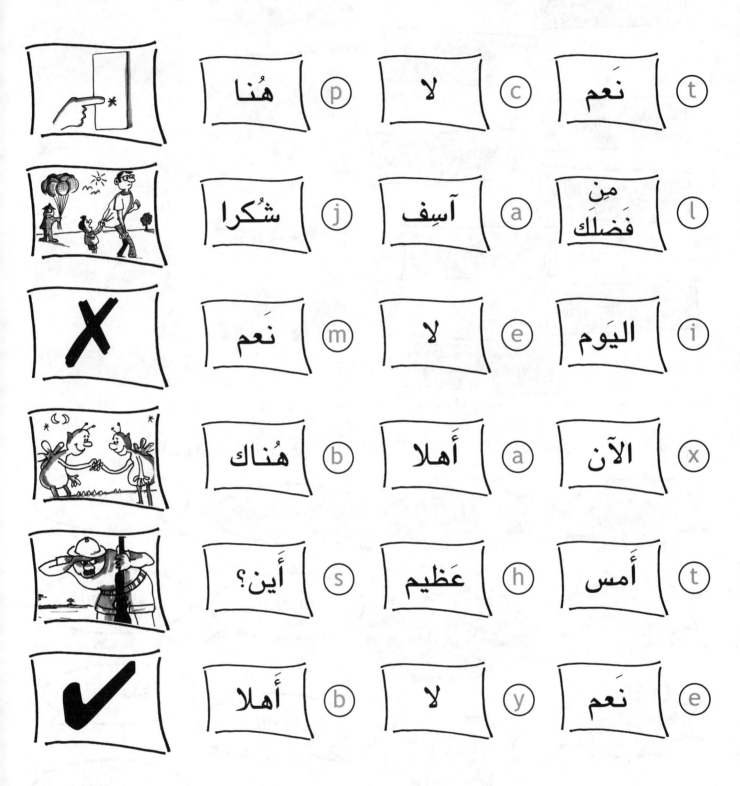

Picture			
	هُنا (p)	لا (c)	نَعم (t)
	شُكرا (j)	آسِف (a)	مِن فَضلك (l)
	نَعم (m)	لا (e)	اليَوم (i)
	هُناك (b)	أَهلا (a)	الآن (x)
	أَين؟ (s)	عَظيم (h)	أَمس (t)
	أَهلا (b)	لا (y)	نَعم (e)

English word: (p) ( ) ( ) ( ) ( ) ( )

What are these people saying? Write the correct number in each speech bubble, as in the example.

© **F**inally, match the Arabic words, their pronunciation, and the English meanings, as in the example.

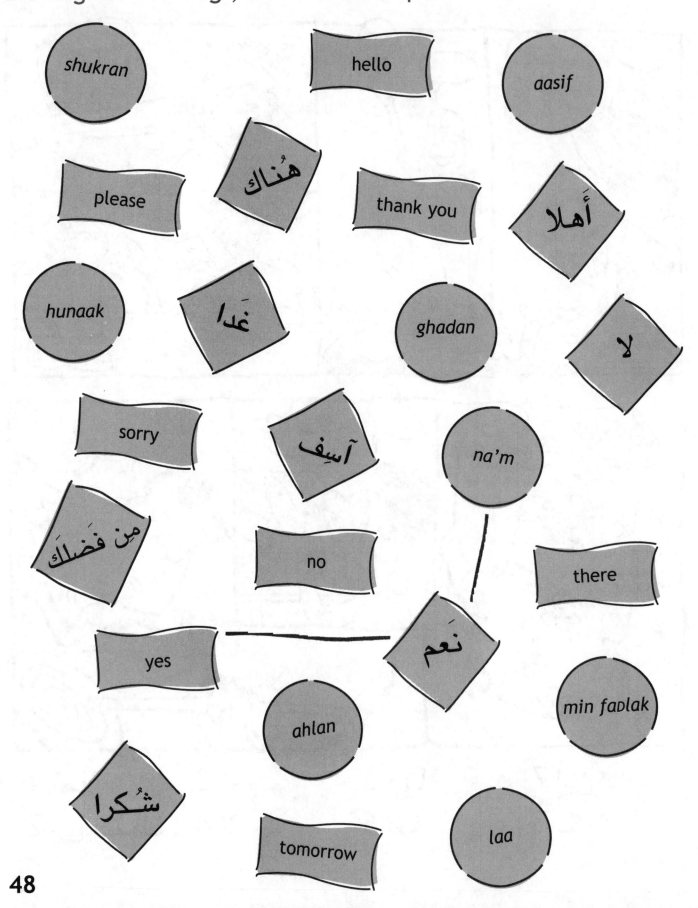

shukran

hello

aasif

هُناك

please

thank you

أَهلا

hunaak

غَدا

ghadan

لا

sorry

آسِف

na'm

مِن فَضلَك

no

there

yes

نَعم

min faᴅlak

ahlan

شُكرا

tomorrow

laa

● ROUND-UP

This section is designed to review all the 100 words you have met in the different topics. It is a good idea to test yourself with your flashcards before trying this section.

◎ These ten objects are hidden in the picture. Can you find and circle them?

كرسي   باب   قبعة   دراجة   سمكة

كلب   سرير   جورب   معطف   وردة

© **S**ee if you can remember all these words.

اليوم

أوتوبيس

سريع

أنف

صحراء

نعم

دولاب

أسد

فستان

رخيص

نهر

ساق

Find the odd one out in these groups of words and say why.

قرد	مائدة	بقرة	كلب

Because it isn't an animal.

- - - - - - - - - - - - - - -

تليفون	قطار	اوتوبيس	سيارة

- - - - - - - - - - - - - - -

جيبة	قميص	معطف	مزرعة

- - - - - - - - - - - - - - -

شجرة	نهر	بحيرة	بحر

- - - - - - - - - - - - - - -

سينما	نظيف	وسخ	غالٍ

- - - - - - - - - - - - - - -

أسد	سمكة	قطة	أرنب

- - - - - - - - - - - - - - -

بطن	رأس	كنبة	ذراع

- - - - - - - - - - - - - - -

غدا	اليوم	أمس	من فضلك

- - - - - - - - - - - - - - -

ثلاجة	دولاب	سرير	فرن

Look at the objects below for 30 seconds.

Cover the picture and try to remember all the objects.
Circle the Arabic words for those you remember.

باب   شكرا   حذاء   وردة

قطار   معطف   هنا   لا   سيارة

حصان   كرسي   جبل   حزام

سرير   عين   تي شيرت   جورب

قرد   تليفزيون   تاكسي   شورت

52

Now match the Arabic words, their pronunciation, and the English meanings, as in the example.

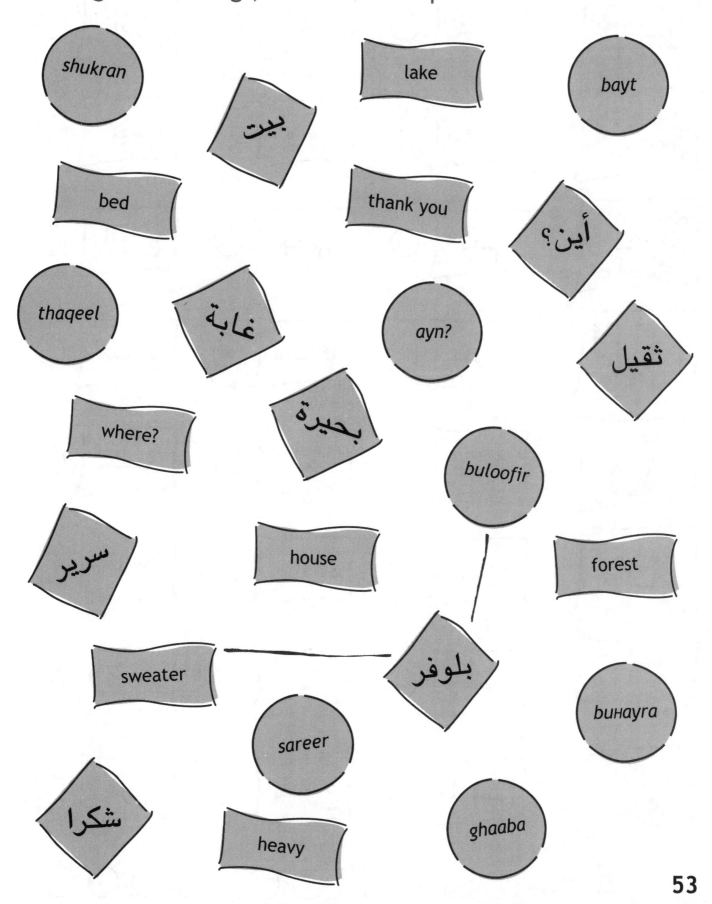

shukran

lake

bayt

بيت

bed

thank you

أين؟

thaqeel

غابة

ayn?

ثقيل

where?

بحيرة

buloofir

house

forest

سرير

sweater

بلوفر

buнayra

sareer

شكرا

heavy

ghaaba

Fill in the English phrase at the bottom of the page.

(w) كنبة	(g) تاكسي	(t) أذن
(o) معطف	(a) وسخ	(e) جسر
(m) نعم	(l) بكم؟	(i) اليوم
(b) بقرة	(l) شباك	(h) مطعم
(e) أين؟	(a) فم	(d) كلب
(o) عين	(p) مائدة	(v) أهلا
(n) تل	(y) لا	(r) اوتوبيس
(n) أرنب	(e) شارع	(s) فرن

54   English phrase: (w) ○ ○ ○   ○ ○ ○ ○ !

Look at the two pictures and check (✔) the objects that are different in Picture B.

 شورت ☐

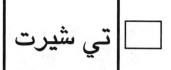 تي شيرت ☐

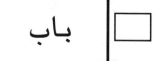 باب ☐

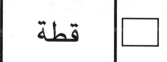 قطة ☐

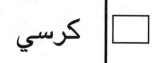 كرسي ☐

 سمكة ☐

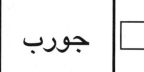 جورب ☐

 كلب ☐

Picture A

Picture B

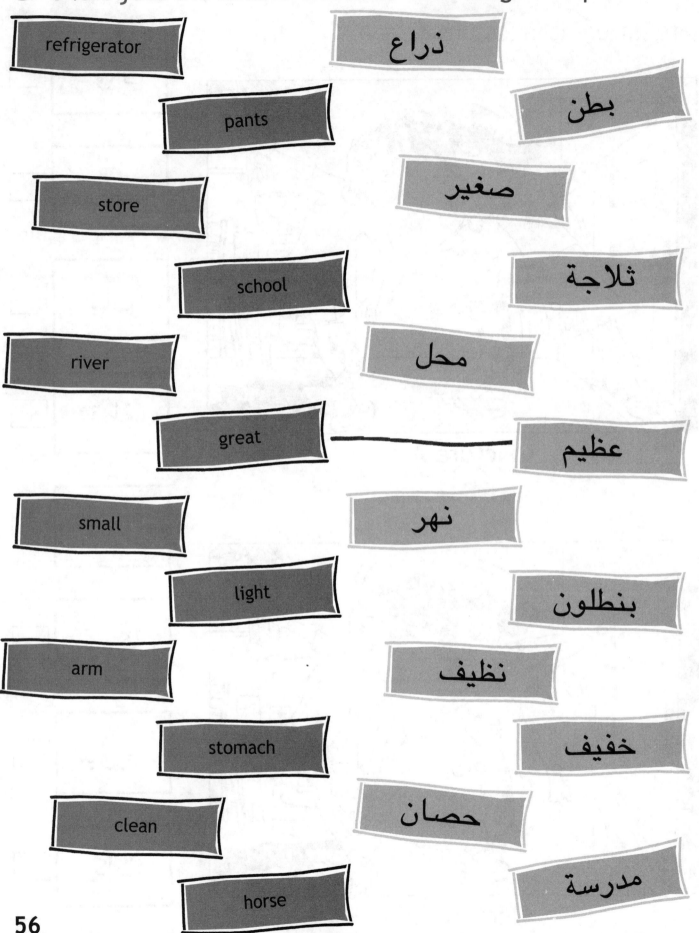

refrigerator

ذراع

pants

بطن

store

صغير

school

ثلاجة

river

محل

great

عظيم

small

نهر

light

بنطلون

arm

نظيف

stomach

خفيف

clean

حصان

horse

مدرسة

56

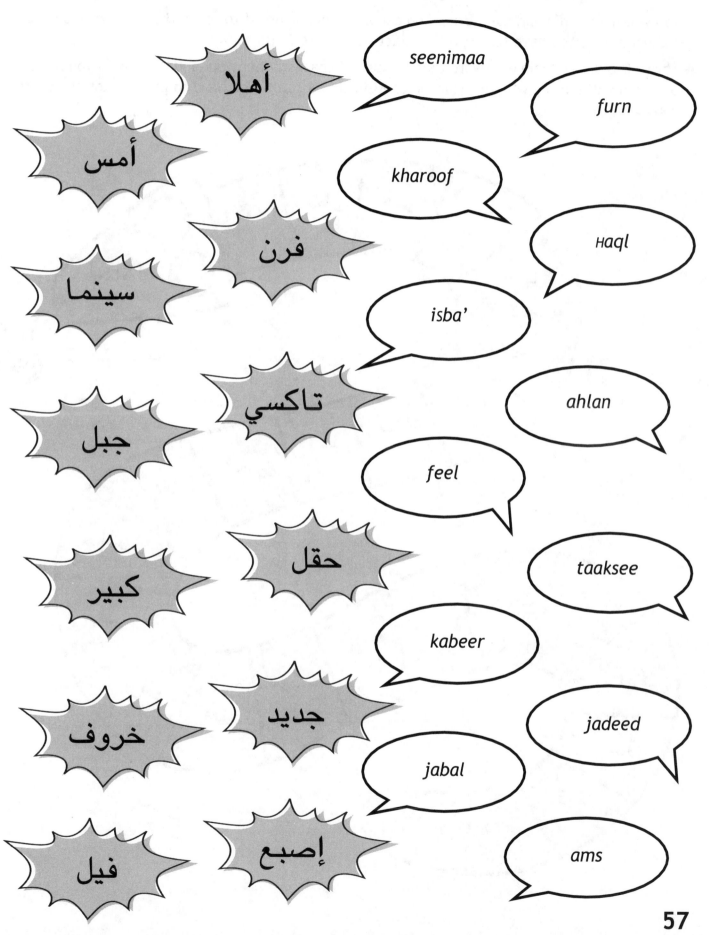

57

Snake game.

- You will need a die and counter(s). You can challenge yourself to reach the finish or play with someone else. You have to throw the exact number to finish.

- Throw the die and move forward that number of spaces. When you land on a word you must pronounce it and say what it means in English. If you can't, you have to go back to the square you came from.

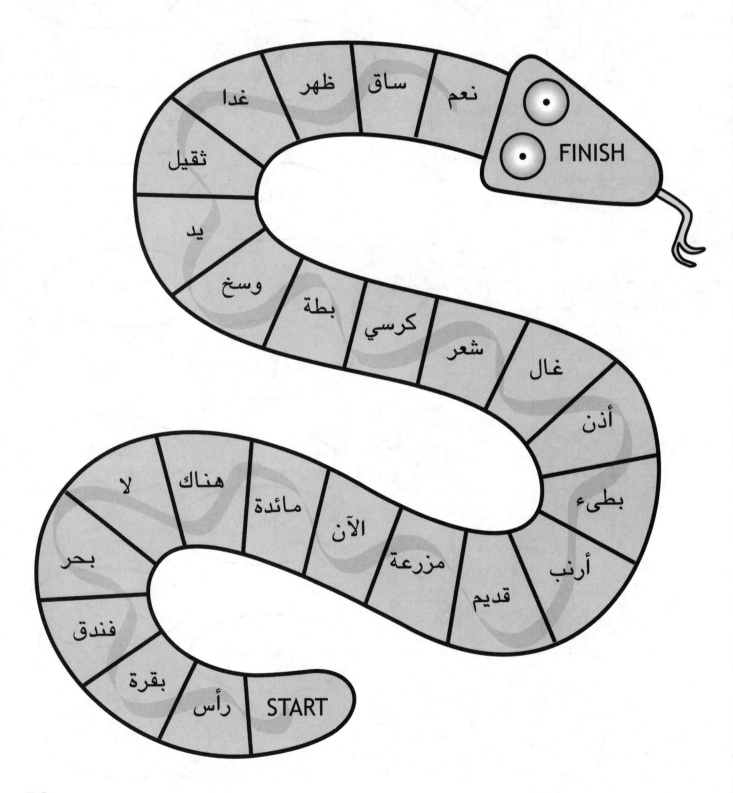

Answers

❶ AROUND THE HOME

Page 10 (top)
See page 9 for correct picture.

Page 10 (bottom)
door	باب
cupboard	دولاب
stove	فرن
bed	سرير
table	مائدة
chair	كرسي
refrigerator	ثلاجة
computer	كمبيوتر

Page 11 (top)
مائدة	*maa-ida*
دولاب	*doolaab*
كمبيوتر	*kumbiyootir*
سرير	*sareer*
شباك	*shubbaak*
تليفون	*tileefoon*
تليفزيون	*tileefizyoon*
كرسي	*kursee*

Page 11 (bottom)

Page 12

Page 13
English word: window

❷ CLOTHES

Page 15 (top)
فستان	*fustaan*
شورت	*shoort*
حذاء	*ниtнaa*
حزام	*нizaam*
قميص	*qamees*
تي شيرت	*tee-sheert*
قبعة	*qubba'a*
جورب	*jawrab*

Page 15 (bottom)

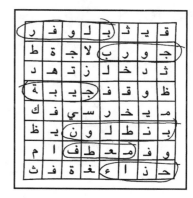

Page 16
hat	قبعة	*qubba'a*
shoe	حذاء	*ниtнaa*
sock	جورب	*jawrab*
shorts	شورت	*shoort*
t-shirt	تي شيرت	*tee-sheert*
belt	حزام	*нizaam*
coat	معطف	*mi'тaf*
pants	بنطلون	*banтaloon*

Page 17
قبعة (hat)	2
معطف (coat)	0
حزام (belt)	2
حذاء (shoe)	2 (1 pair)
بنطلون (pants)	0
شورت (shorts)	2
فستان (dress)	1
جورب (sock)	6 (3 pairs)
جيبة (skirt)	1
تي شيرت (t-shirt)	3
قميص (shirt)	0
بلوفر (sweater)	1

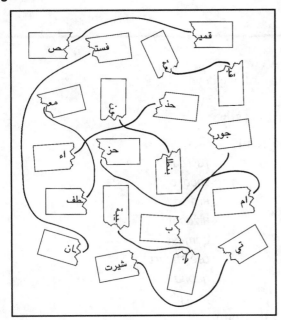

❸ AROUND TOWN

Page 20 (top)

movie theater	سينما
store	محل
hotel	فندق
taxi	تاكسي
car	سيارة
train	قطار
school	مدرسة
house	بيت

Page 20 (bottom)

bicycle	4
taxi	7
house	2
train	6
bus	1
road	3
car	5

Page 21

مدرسة   تاكسي   اوتوبيس

سيارة   قطار   مطعم

فندق   دراجة

Page 22

English word: school

Page 23

اوتوبيس	*ootoobees*
تاكسي	*taaksee*
مدرسة	*madrasa*
سيارة	*sayyaara*
فندق	*funduq*
بيت	*bayt*
دراجة	*darraaja*
قطار	*qiτaar*
محل	*maнall*
سينما	*seenimaa*
مطعم	*maτ'am*
شارع	*shaari'*

❹ COUNTRYSIDE

Page 25

See page 24 for correct picture.

Page 26

جسر	✔	حقل	✔
شجرة	✔	غابة	✘
صحراء	✘	بحيرة	✘
تل	✘	نهر	✔
جبل	✔	وردة	✔
بحر	✘	مزرعة	✔

Page 27 (top)

جبل	*jabal*
نهر	*nahr*
غابة	*ghaaba*
صحراء	*saнraa*
بحر	*baнr*
مزرعة	*mazra'a*
جسر	*jisr*
حقل	*наql*

Page 27 (bottom)

ن	ي	د	ث	ب	س	و	ف	ه
ج	خ	و	ب	ش	ر	ة	ر	
ث	و	ر	د	ة	ه	ت	د	ث
ث	ظ	و	ق	ب	ي	د	ح	ق
ث	م	ز	ر	ع	ة	ي	ق	
ت	ل	ظ	ب	و	ن	د	ي	ف
و	ف	م	ق	ط	غ	ا	م	
ض	ذ	ا	ج	س	ر	م	ب	

Page 28

sea	بحر	*baнr*
lake	بحيرة	*buнayra*
desert	صحراء	*saнraa*
farm	مزرعة	*mazra'a*
flower	وردة	*warda*
mountain	جبل	*jabal*
river	نهر	*nahrr*
field	حقل	*нaql*

❺ OPPOSITES

Page 30

expensive	غال
big	كبير
light	خفيف
slow	بطىء
clean	نظيف
inexpensive	رخيص
dirty	وسخ
small	صغير
heavy	ثقيل
new	جديد
fast	سريع
old	قديم

Page 31

English word: change

Page 32

Odd one outs are those which are not opposites:

ثقيل
صغير
جديد
وسخ
بطىء
رخيص

Page 33

old	جديد
big	صغير
new	قديم
slow	سريع
dirty	نظيف
small	كبير
heavy	خفيف
clean	وسخ
light	ثقيل
expensive	رخيص
inexpensive	غال

❻ ANIMALS

Page 35

بقرة أرنب سمكة أسد

خروف كلب قرد

حصان فأر قطة

Page 36

أرنب	*arnab*
حصان	*нusaan*
قرد	*qird*
كلب	*kalb*
قطة	*qiтта*
فأر	*faar*
بطة	*baтта*
سمكة	*samaka*
أسد	*asad*
خروف	*kharoof*
بقرة	*baqara*
فيل	*feel*

Page 37

elephant	✔	mouse	✘
monkey	✘	cat	✔
sheep	✔	dog	✘
lion	✔	cow	✔
fish	✔	horse	✘
duck	✘	rabbit	✔

Page 38

monkey	قرد
cow	بقرة
mouse	فأر
dog	كلب
sheep	خروف
fish	سمكة
lion	أسد
elephant	فيل
cat	قطة
duck	بطة
rabbit	أرنب
horse	حصان

❼ PARTS OF THE BODY

Page 40

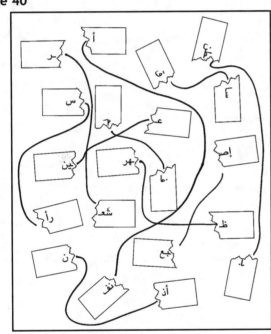

Page 41 (top)

You should have also drawn pictures of:

leg; mouth; ear; nose; eye; hair

62

Page 41 (bottom)

رأس	*ra-as*
أذن	*uтhun*
بطن	*baтn*
أنف	*anf*
ذراع	*тhiraa*
فم	*fam*
عين	*'ayn*
ظهر	*zahr*

Page 42

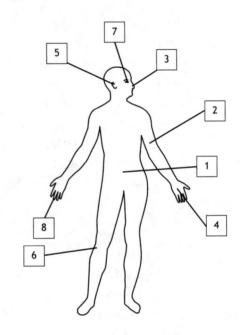

1.	بطن	*baтn*
2.	ذراع	*тhiraa*
3.	أنف	*anf*
4.	يد	*yad*
5.	أذن	*uтhun*
6.	ساق	*saaq*
7.	عين	*'ayn*
8.	أصبع	*isba'*

Page 43

ear	أذن	*uтhun*
hair	شعر	*sha'r*
hand	يد	*yad*
stomach	بطن	*baтn*
arm	ذراع	*тhiraa*
back	ظهر	*zahr*
finger	أصبع	*isba'*
leg	ساق	*saaq*

⑧ USEFUL EXPRESSIONS

Page 45 (top)

great	عظيم
yes	نعم
yesterday	أمس
where?	أين؟
today	اليوم
here	هنا
please	من فضلك
no	لا

Page 45 (bottom)

هناك	hunaak
أهلا	ahlan
غدا	ghadan
مع السلامة	ma' as-salaama
بكم؟	bikam?
شكرا	shukran
آسف	aasif
عظيم	'azeem

Page 46

English word: please

Page 47

Page 48

yes	نعم	na'm
hello	أهلا	ahlan
no	لا	laa
sorry	آسف	aasif
please	من فضلك	min faɒlak
there	هناك	hunaak
thank you	شكرا	shukran
tomorrow	غدا	ghadan

● ROUND-UP

Page 49

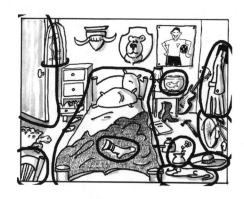

Page 50

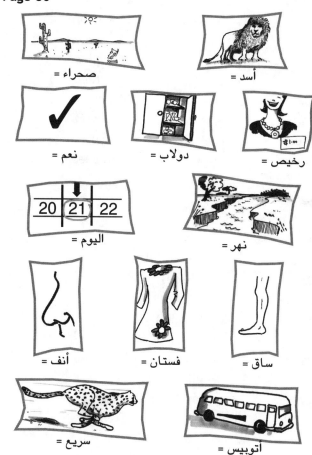

صحراء =   أسد =

نعم =   دولاب =   رخيص =

اليوم =   نهر =

أنف =   فستان =   ساق =

سريع =   أتوبيس =

Page 51

مائدة (Because it isn't an animal.)

تليفون (Because it isn't a means of transportation.)

مزرعة (Because it isn't an item of clothing.)

شجرة (Because it isn't connected with water.)

سينما (Because it isn't a descriptive word.)

سمكة (Because it lives in water/doesn't have legs.)

كنبة (Because it isn't a part of the body.)

من فضلك (Because it isn't an expression of time.)

سرير (Because you wouldn't find it in the kitchen.)

63

Page 52

Words that appear in the picture:

تي شيرت

سيارة

وردة

حذاء

قطار

قرد

تليفزيون

كرسي

حزام

شورت

Page 53

sweater	بلوفر	*buloofir*
lake	بحيرة	*buнayra*
thank you	شكرا	*shukran*
bed	سرير	*sareer*
house	بيت	*bayt*
forest	غابة	*ghaaba*
where?	أين؟	*ayn*
heavy	ثقيل	*thaqeel*

Page 54

English phrase: well done!

Page 55

شورت	✔ (shade)
تي شيرت	✘
باب	✔ (handle)
قطة	✘
كرسي	✔ (back)
سمكة	✔ (direction)
جورب	✔ (pattern)
كلب	✘

Page 56

refrigerator	ثلاجة
pants	بنطلون
store	محل
school	مدرسة
river	نهر
great	عظيم
small	صغير
light	خفيف
arm	ذراع
stomach	بطن
clean	نظيف
horse	حصان

Page 57

أهلا	*ahlan*
أمس	*ams*
فرن	*furn*
سينما	*seenimaa*
تاكسي	*taaksee*
جبل	*jabal*
حقل	*нaql*
كبير	*kabeer*
جديد	*jadeed*
خروف	*kharoof*
إصبع	*isba'*
فيل	*feel*

Page 58

Here are the English equivalents and pronunciation of the words, in order from START to FINISH:

head *ra-as*	farm *mazra'a*	duck *baтта*
cow *baqara*	old *qadeem*	dirty *wasikh*
hotel *funduq*	rabbit *arnab*	hand *yad*
sea *baнr*	slow *baтee*	heavy *thaqeel*
no *laa*	ear *uтнun*	tomorrow *ghadan*
there *hunaak*	expensive *ghalee*	back *zahr*
table *maa-ida*	hair *sha'r*	leg *saaq*
now *al-aan*	chair *kursee*	yes *na'm*

شباك

shubbaak

كمبيوتر

kumbiyootir

دولاب

doolaab

مائدة

maa-ida

كرسي

kursee

ثلاجة

thallaaja

فرن

furn

كنبة

kanaba

سرير

sareer

باب

baab

تليفزيون

tileefizyoon

تليفون

tileefoon

window	computer
cupboard	table
chair	refrigerator
stove	sofa
bed	door
television	telephone

معطف

mi'ꭲaf

حزام

ꭹizaam

قبعة

qubba'a

جيبة

jeeba

حذاء

ꭹiꭲꭲaa

تي شيرت

tee-sheert

قميص

qamees

بلوفر

buloofir

جورب

jawrab

شورت

shoort

فستان

fustaan

بنطلون

banꭲaloon

coat	belt
hat	skirt
shoe	t-shirt
shirt	sweater
sock	shorts
dress	pants

مدرسة

madrasa

سيارة

sayyaara

شارع

shaari'

سينما

seenimaa

فندق

funduq

محل

maнall

تاكسي

taaksee

دراجة

darraaja

مطعم

maт'am

أوتوبيس

ootoobees

قطار

qiтaar

بيت

bayt

car	school
movie theater	road
store	hotel
bicycle	taxi
bus	restaurant
house	train

غابة

ghaaba

بحيرة

buнayra

بحر

baнr

تل

tal

شجرة

shajara

جبل

jabal

وردة

warda

صحراء

saнraa

نهر

nahr

جسر

jisr

حقل

наql

مزرعة

mazra'a

forest	lake
sea	hill
tree	mountain
flower	desert
river	bridge
field	farm

ثقيل

thaqeel

خفيف

khafeef

كبير

kabeer

صغير

sagheer

قديم

qadeem

جديد

jadeed

سريع

saree'

بطيء

baтee

نظيف

nazeef

وسخ

wasikh

رخيص

rakhees

غالٍ

ghaalee

light	heavy
small	big
new	old
slow	fast
dirty	clean
expensive	cheap

بطة
baтta

قطة
qiтta

فأر
faar

بقرة
baqara

أرنب
arnab

كلب
kalb

حصان
нusaan

قرد
qird

أسد
asad

سمكة
samaka

فيل
feel

خروف
kharoof

cat	duck
cow	mouse
dog	rabbit
monkey	horse
fish	lion
sheep	elephant

ذراع
THiraa'

إصبع
isba'

رأس
ra-as

فم
fam

أذن
UTHUn

ساق
saaq

يد
yad

بطن
baTn

عين
'ayn

شعر
sha'r

أنف
anf

ظهر
zahr

finger	arm
mouth	head
leg	ear
stomach	hand
hair	eye
back	nose

شكرا	من فضلك
shukran	*min faDlak*

لا	نعم
laa	*na'm*

مع السلامة	أهلا
ma' as-salaama	*ahlan*

اليوم	أمس
al-yaum	*ams*

أين؟	غداً
ayn	*ghadan*

هناك	هنا
hunaak	*huna*

بكم؟	آسف
bikam	*aasif*

الآن	عظيم!
al-aan	*'azeem*

thank you	please
no	yes
goodbye	hello
today	yesterday
where?	tomorrow
there	here
how much?	sorry!
now	great!